Letters from the Elements

DE LITERAE ELEMENTIS

Letters from the Elements

DE LITERAE ELEMENTIS

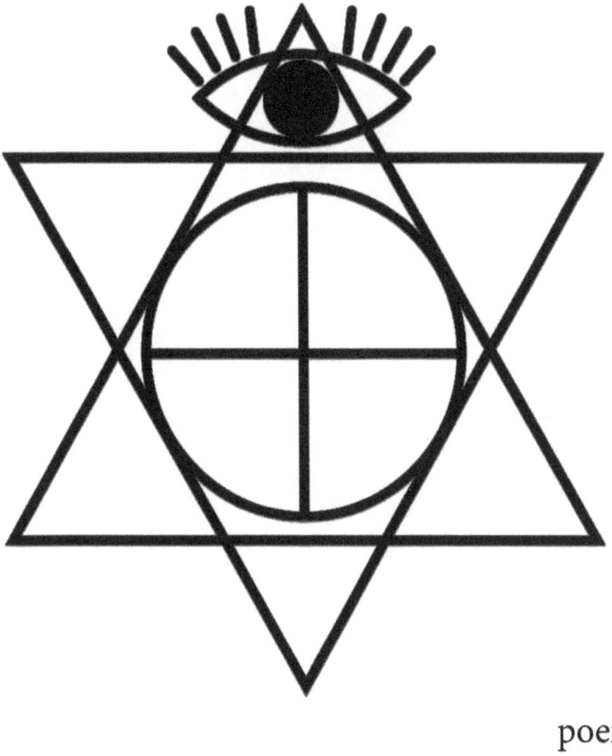

poems
by
MONZIE LEO

copyright 2020 Monzie Leo

cover design: Michelle Tschetter

ISBN: 978-1-950380-88-6

LLOC: 2020931584

Stubborn Mule Press

Devil's Elbow, MO

stubbornmulepress.com

TABLE OF CONTENTS

Songs of Water

Grace the Blues	13
Winter's First	15
Leaves That Sparkle	16
For Pangea	18
Quintessence; Æther	19

Songs of Fire

Harbinger of Will	27
Homunculus	28
Earrach	29
Chained to The Bottom of The Ocean	30

Letters from Earth

What You Seek is Seeking You	35
Groveling Nothing	36
Get Fantastic!	38

Notes from Air

Marigold Skies	43
Invariable Grit	45
A Decree of Love	46

Dedicated to my old friend and sunshine:
PANGEA KALI VIRGA

Songs of Water

Water is related to adaptability of the Soul. Water works in contrast or against the rigidity of the Air. We must shape the mind to fit the circumstances and this tests our altruism and our philanthropy.

—Gnosis: The Four Ideals

Grace the Blues

I could
in good conscience
learn to love again

not today

a dream
in everything
in this
our symbols of dawn
our mutual tyranny
our haphazard filth

the gyroscope you
whippingly die for
when you glide like The Goddess
across the stage
of the cherished
and woeful
and desolate
razor

I never said I was courageous
just ready
ready to find you
or to assume at the least
we could have a stable
and regular being

how I'd give it a go

or let it touch me
like a long lost ambition

how we could watch ourselves
crush each other
in this demonic trust of cohesive bliss

how it leads us to nothing
or to the perfect nothing

how we could grace
the blues with a staff

of grudges

Winter's First

could you believe there are colder days to come?

the spring and summer gone for now
you were home to the daddy long legs
now the downy woodpeckers
flock to your
hanging seed

a marsh unfrozen is a bath house
for cardinals and the like

still no snow touches the muddy ground
red leaves like loose teeth
tremble from the cherry saplings
without wonder or care
of the rabbits
or the doe that dare
starvingly consume them

the wind bustles
with the constant threat

of winter's first

Leaves That Sparkle

emboldened and fierce
the moonlit night
these
stars may be leaves
these leaves may be stars
on a dewy soft ground

the frosted glass
awakens
more of this light
it is asked to be brighter
as it passes through
it is begged to be illuminated
as it crests

the osage trees cradle the stars above
long curling limbs hold dying foliage
one sways
one blinks
or is that what it is?

the glaze on my window
makes cascading fixtures
of the night sky

to it I am emboldened
it is fierce
this moonlit night

these stars maybe leaves
dangling from branches
these leaves maybe stars
on a dewy soft ground

For Pangaea

you have my loyalty
my affection
therefore my love

for as long as i can last
for as long as one of us
has feet
on this earth
as long as we are chained to this existence
bound by this gravity

from the nothing we will both become
in our souls' next lives
the time after that

as an earthworm
a snowflake

let me dance in your heart
as you dance in mine

you magnificent star

Quintessence; Æther

Advice 1

what rhythms
do teach you
the regular qualm

unguarded futures?
or opportunities projection?

any two circumstances
or a scolded rose
can show you well
the scent of success

though introduce you better
to the acrid stench
of progress

Advice 2

whenever our
deeds are
structured to
provide insight

we act as a root system
for others to grow
filament for others
to spark

an idiot for an
idiot to loathe

Advice 3

the urge
overwhelming
took him
with great ease
and tenacity

he then spoke of worlds not unlike his own
very consciousness

he erupted to the notion
that not all things are solid
or even relevant

moot
simply put

nothing

and therefore just right

Advice 4

A life alone
soldered and
garnished
with aching prosperity
so well adjusted

newness beckons
a tearfully
terrorized eye

so churns apathy like
slow tasting, passionate
butter

the grade abundant

as true pleasure
escapes our quality
it leaves fruitful
trees dying
shifting an essence around
like a mouth, bitter
with too much fat

Advice 5

once these horn trumpets played happy tunes
now wooden fingers play nothing
a once amalgamation of love
now gone completely
awry
now this radiant glow ensues
a philosophy deterred from goodness
it insures a lack of flow
from one's heart
to one's crown
a binding circle
explosions verbose
and without tangible references

SONGS OF FIRE

The candidate is exposed to the ordeal to examine his serenity and sweetness. The wrathful and choleric inevitably fail this ordeal. The candidate experiences being persecuted, insulted, wronged, etc.

—Samael Aur Weor

Harbinger of Will

without fury of the damned
we are forsaken
gods and royalty
born to be free
each passing day
blackened by night
vituperation
an angel of light
life without hesitation

Homunculus

do you speak
the language of energy?
how is it that i have come to be?
my creators are my parents
and so on

my grief stricken woes
are ardent and rest gently
on my disgust
in the same way a legible face
cannot lie

was my shallow heart inherited?
was my stiff neck?

old visceral tones rumble
through my every choice
the daylight fleets again
in and out of cold and dark
it returns
like i will
to nothing

remnants of this being
shattered
torn
and lost

Earrach

a grand murder of crows
one thousand of them

they fly deep beneath
the winter's cloud

it's sullen darkness
brings a promise of spring
the rain
the budding babes
the everlasting want

burn the dead trees
you decorated them
call on the great Tree spirit
they are the standing people
ask them to come home

revel in the numbing wind
let it stifle your place of being
and defeat you

birds chirp
the eternal morning waxes
your breath
is every season
every morning

Chained to the Bottom of the Ocean

when gravity subsides
and chains succeed
from their heavy captors
unbound, unburdened
with the strength
of giants
inured to remain
broken
under
weighted cinder
plummeting iron
abyssal shackles
and eyes turned translucent
with truth rebounded
in shadow's wake
breath frozen in time, drifting upwards
at mass' abhorrent end
sheathed in an unholy pressure
crushed
under the weight
of æons

LETTERS FROM EARTH

We must learn how to take advantage of the worst adversities.
The worst adversities bring us the best opportunities.
We must learn to smile before all adversities.
This is the Law. Those who succumb to pain
before adversities of existence cannot
victoriously pass the ordeal of Earth.

—Samael Aun Weor

What You Seek is Seeking You

as in nature things that are alike
grow to look alike
this kindredness has been seeking me
as I have been seeking it

the shattering veil
between us two
beckons our tomorrow
it begs us
as if our anticipation
is grifted by our interest to join each other

in this traipsing physical dialogue
in this palace of our love
the crepuscular glisten of our bodies
I jaunt amongst you
championed by the sheer and ebullient crest
of our will to please one another
let me open you up
as the aphids do the peony

let me learn from you
let me live in your cascading goodness

Groveling Nothing

who created this groveling?
who took this cheese grater
placed it gently
on the fronts of these teeth
then began to sway gingerly
as if to request
it go painless

as if to demand
you ever had it at all;
that the old sanity return

this cyclical turmoil
runs burdens

the patriarch of an everlasting
heap of steaming
putrid
waste

unfortunate to the student
who is massacred only by
the waxing anxiety
of a staunch myopia

fortified by a thicket of thorns
and distrust
and pure hatred
for what the old man has done

how forgiving

for who they are
means to serve
how showing love
is volcanic

thick and grieving
the loss of perspective

allowing it to wane into the great nothing
to be the sea

to change a notion
to conquer another day

or to have a day be worth conquering
to create our own groveling

Get Fantastic!

it is in this moment
I declare my
fed-up-ed-ness
my eternal frustration
my super natural ability to be depressed
or sad
it is in this moment
I declare
I leave these habits to wolves
better suited
to carry the weight of madness
and insecurity
it is by this notion
that I will continue to maintain
an air of happiness
good will and faith
regarding my fellow two leggeds
my four leggeds as well
I will no longer hold a candle
to insanity

all creation
should benefit
from everyone's good grace
that good grace
should soon become inherent
with this agreeable notion!
with this enhancing declaration!
to live this moment constantly
to heed to its results

with more of the same grand good grace
that ushers Oh! So many!
to an echelon of supreme understanding
and assured Fantastickisms!

torrid woes
of past crinkled thoughts
fail to compare!
my happiness
is my mind's response
to everything it sees
and will continue to see!
for judgement's inability to love
plagues us with distracting
and unnecessary evil
now hear!
I declare my happiness
to no longer lack length
and need not compensation for altitude!
to love and to hold this universe
in my arms
to enjoy its lowly repetitions
petty and insecure
Ecclesiastically!
accepting its flaws

Worshiping its holy nature
mediocres
terribles
bads
goods
and greats

Notes from Air

Air is the mobility of the Soul. Our attachments are tested, and in this type of ordeal there is a real temptation to catastrophize.

—Gnosis: The Four Ideals

Marigold Skies

we told each other our mother's dreams
under marigold skies

we told each other
the names we kept to ourselves

the deeds of friendship we hold
the righteousness we cradle

we told each other our mother's dreams
under marigold skies

we told each other the names
the names
we kept to ourselves

we asked daringly and received
we held hands as beating hearts
we danced around our burning intention
in fire
we lifted each other up

held hands

our passion beats
it is rolling thunder

we told the marigold skies
our mother's dreams
then watched fruition glow

under that gleaming wax
we championed our goals, our fears

we told each other
our mother's names
under marigold skies
we told each other
the dreams we kept to ourselves

held our passions
as roaring thunder
we asked daringly and received
watched fruition glow
under that
gleaming wax

a long enraptured nautilus in limestone
we championed our egos
to look inside one another's ribcages

to live inside one another's hearts

Invariable Grit

wavering and gaunt
watching an insect cold
we can wallow and revel too
in its simple adherent complexion
diving, diving, diving…
into its abhorrent scheme;

a grift like no other.
journeying into likeness,
as if this churlish tenacity's place
was peppered with air
or given enough time to yield
to all dying geniuses grand graceful goodness.

a moment in time
free from that ghastly
ever present
charmless
beholdened
touch of tear

we float and walk
as children
ready to die

A Decree of Love

it's the least one could do
for the ripple in the streams
as I've been gone far to long

the stars they appear
falling from dreams, sometimes hopeless
and wishes fade like the dawn

the moon comes out waxing
waning, full or brightless
certain you'll never do me wrong

when lovers stress over
matters often chilling
madness is bound to take its toll

if darkness triumphs
in a world filled with doubt
my open arms will be your throne

I'll be here waiting
over time and time again
as long as our burdens we'll share
you've seen me fret
you know whom I loath
you're as steadfastly stubborn as I
for life my love
you I will cherish
through the end of earth and time

a world ever fragile
oft torn asunder by such greatness
could rip and with each other
we'd be fine

I'll bequeath to you courage
you'll give unto me rationality
as spring blossoms bloom

Oh! sweeping clouds
how morning's dawn defines you
we embrace the encircling moon

Monzie Leo is an occult poet that emphasizes the Bardic tradition. A troubadour by rite, they have recorded several albums with their country band The Big Sky. They live in the woods in a home they built from scraps.

www.ingramcontent.com/pod-product-compliance
Lightning Source LLC
Chambersburg PA
CBHW030140100526
44592CB00011B/984